Don't Stress You're Blessed

Written by TaNaa' Griffin

Illustration by
Jasmine T. Mills

Editor: Sam Meyer

Dedication

When you become a dad one day, keep this book as a reminder that you can achieve at parenting.

About The Author

Hey there! I'm a daughter of God, housewife, homeschool mom, sister, and friend. I earned my bachelor of science in Social Work at Spalding University in 2015. While studying I met some great people, especially by connecting with three caring organizations - Special Olympics Kentucky, Best Buddies Kentucky, and The Sisters of Charity of Nazareth - that show the importance of being compassionate towards others and practicing self-care. I live to serve my Lord and Savior Jesus Christ and to love His people. Spreading joy and encouragement is my goal. The ups and downs of parenthood inspired me to write this comforting book of inspiration for all parents. I want to encourage not only parents but everyone to not be so hard on themselves. I hope that readers will enjoy my first book, *Don't Stress You're Blessed,* and the next books to come. With much love, TaNaa' Alexia Griffin.

Introduction

This book is love bundled in a warm fuzzy hug for parents who are worrying about their child's development. When it comes to growth there is no race. All children shine in their own way. They all have gifts to contribute to this world in need. This is a Christian-based comforting book for adults designed like a children's book to reach the inner child of readers. My prayer is that this book brings sunshine to parents on tough days and gives them a pep in their step to keep going on their parenting journey.

Are you worried about your little one?

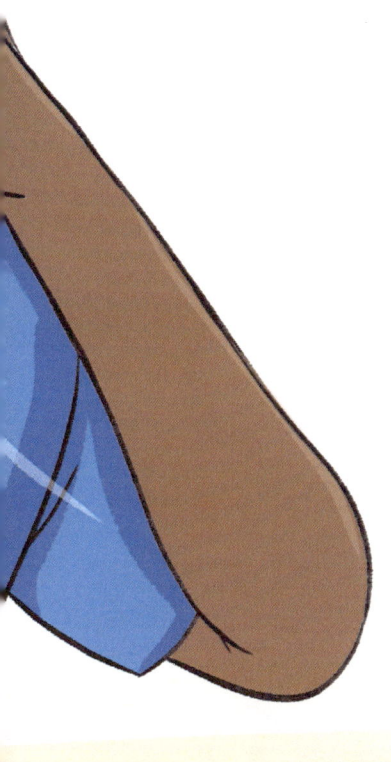

Take a deep breath and chill hun.
They are healthy and alive, just sit
back and watch them thrive.

I know what you're thinking,
it's easier said than done.

Ask yourself, does it make it any better when you keep comparing your child to other little ones?

Every child is unique from the way that they communicate to the foods that they eat.

In The Good Lord's eyes, they are already made whole and complete.

No reason to harp on negativity it
can stunt your child's creativity.

Remember that your kids can feel your energy, be their peace not their enemy.

Choose not to stress on the time table.

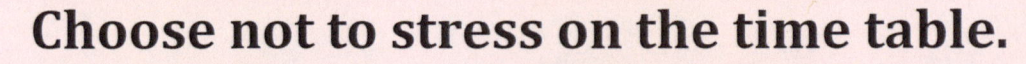

What really matters is that one
day they will be able.

Don't get caught up in the not yet,
why not, and why me.

Tell your thoughts to hush up please! God's not finished carving His masterpiece.

Still don't believe me? That your child couldn't ever achieve at A.B.C.D.E.F.or G.?

Think back to Jesus at Calvary His story
ended in the ultimate victory.

Cheer on their gifts and speak
life to their strengths.

Stay positive in every stage even through the toils, tides, and rifts.

Kids grow up fast soon you'll see. Time will roll by and flee in maximum speed.

Don't miss out on the fun with your little one.
Their journey in life has only just begun.

Now that you've gradu-ated from this overthinking class, praise God that the troubles that clouded your eyes won't last.

You can stop worrying now, go on and hug your sweet little child. The End.

www.ingramcontent.com/pod-product-compliance
Lightning Source LLC
Chambersburg PA
CBRC090832120626
46547CB00008B/663